D1517359

Iguanodon

by Daniel Cohen

Consultant:
Brent Breithaupt
Director
Geological Museum
University of Wyoming

Bridgestone Books
an imprint of Capstone Press
Mankato, Minnesota

Bridgestone Books are published by Capstone Press
151 Good Counsel Drive, P.O. Box 669, Mankato, Minnesota 56002
http://www.capstone-press.com

Library of Congress Cataloging-in-Publication Data
Cohen, Daniel, 1936–
    Iguanodon / by Daniel Cohen.
    p. cm.—(Discovering dinosaurs)
    Summary: Describes what is known of the physical characteristics, behavior, and habitat
of this plant-eating dinosaur.
    Includes bibliographical references and index.
    ISBN 0-7368-1623-2 (hardcover)
    1. Iguanodon--Juvenile literature. [1. Iguanodon. 2. Dinosaurs.] I. Title.
QE862.O65 C614 2003
567.914—dc21   2002010715

Editorial Credits
Erika Shores, editor; Karen Risch, product planning editor; Linda Clavel, series designer;
    Patrick D. Dentinger, cover production designer; Angi Gahler, production artist;
    Alta Schaffer, photo researcher

Photo Credits
Hulton/Archive Photos by Getty Images, 16
Index Stock Imagery/RO-MA Stock, 6
The Natural History Museum, cover, 1, 8, 10, 18, 20; J. Sibbick, 4; Orbis, 12

1 2 3 4 5 6 08 07 06 05 04 03

Table of Contents

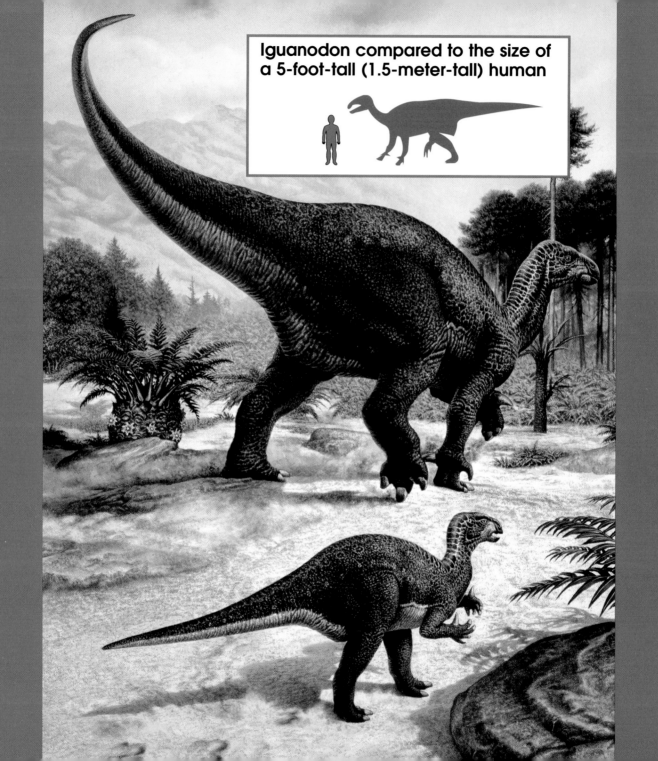

Iguanodon compared to the size of a 5-foot-tall (1.5-meter-tall) human

Iguanodon

Iguanodon (i-GWA-no-DON) was a plant-eating dinosaur. It was one of the first dinosaurs ever discovered. Iguanodon lived about 130 million years ago. Its name means "iguana tooth." Iguanodon was 20 feet (6 meters) long. It weighed 2 to 3 tons (1.8 to 2.7 metric tons).

iguana
a large lizard

The World of Iguanodon

Earth looked different during the time Iguanodon lived. Earth's landmasses were closer together. Earth's climate was warm and wet. Giant ferns and other tropical plants covered the land.

tropical
related to warm and wet weather

Ouranosaurus was a relative of Iguanodon. Both Ouranosaurus and Iguanodon were iguanodontids.

Iguanodon belonged to a group of dinosaurs called iguanodontids. These plant-eating dinosaurs usually walked on two legs. Ouranosaurus (oh-RAN-oh-SORE-us) was an iguanodontid that lived during the time of Iguanodon.

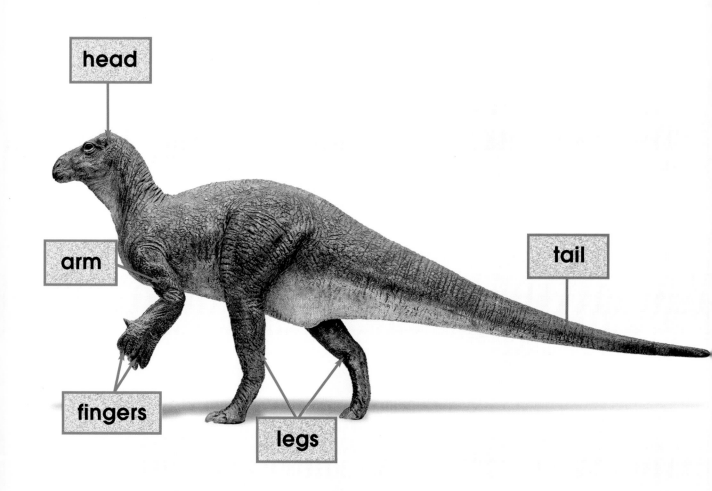

head

arm

tail

fingers

legs

Parts of Iguanodon

Iguanodon was a large dinosaur. It stood up to 17 feet (5 meters) tall on two strong legs. Iguanodon's feet had three toes. Its arms had five-fingered hands. Its thumbs were spikes. Iguanodon had a long, stiff tail.

What Iguanodon Ate

Iguanodon was a herbivore. It ate only plants. It did not have front teeth. Iguanodon used its bony beak to tear leaves off plants. The teeth on the sides of its mouth were large and strong. Iguanodon used these teeth to chew the leaves.

ENGLAND

BELGIUM

GERMANY

FRANCE

SPAIN

TUNISIA

South Dakota

Utah

UNITED STATES

Areas where Iguanodon
fossils have been found

Discovering Iguanodon

In 1822, Mary Ann Mantell found large teeth by a roadside in southeast England. Mary Ann gave the teeth to her husband, Dr. Gideon Mantell. He was interested in fossils. Gideon thought the teeth looked like iguana teeth. He called the animal the teeth came from "Iguanodon."

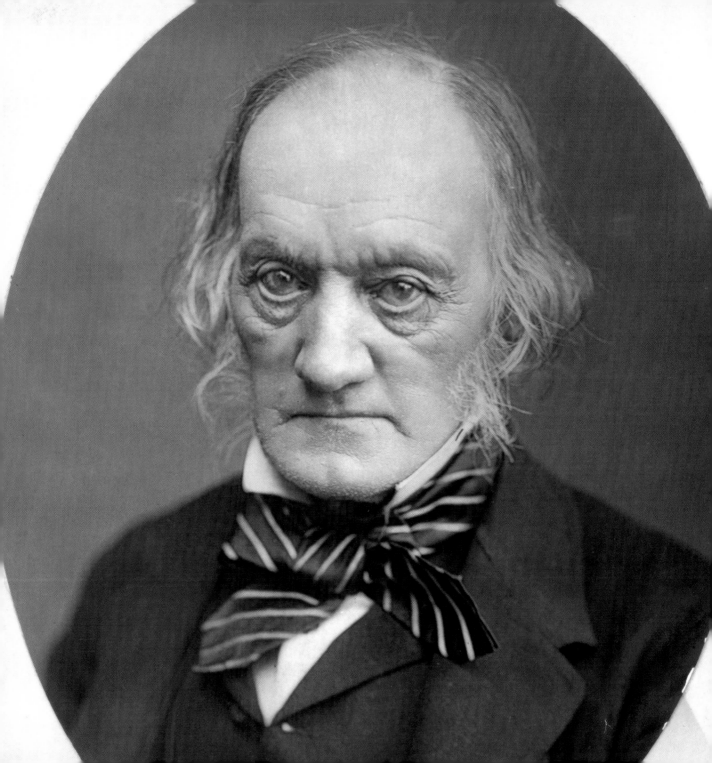

Richard Owen

In 1842, British scientist Richard Owen studied Iguanodon. He realized it was not just a giant lizard. He said it belonged to a group of huge reptiles. These reptiles lived long ago and were now extinct. Richard called these reptiles "dinosaurs." Dinosaur means "terrible lizard."

extinct
no longer living anywhere in the world

Iguanodon teeth

Making Iguanodon

Richard tried to imagine what Iguanodon looked like. He made a model from the few Iguanodon teeth and bones he had. His first model made Iguanodon look like a giant rhinoceros. People later found complete Iguanodon skeletons. Richard created better models based on these skeletons.

Studying Iguanodon Today

Today, paleontologists continue to study Iguanodon fossils. Some scientists think Iguanodon walked on all four legs at times. Paleontologists also think Iguanodons traveled together in herds.

paleontologist
a scientist who finds and studies fossils

Hands On: Make a Dinosaur

At first, people knew little about what dinosaurs looked like. People made drawings of how they thought a dinosaur may have looked. Some of these early drawings and models looked very strange. Try this activity to make a dinosaur drawing.

What You Need

A sheet of paper
A pencil
Three friends
Tape

What You Do

1. Tear the paper into three equal parts.
2. Give one piece of the paper to one friend. Ask him or her to draw the head of a dinosaur. Do not let the other two friends see the drawing.
3. Give another piece of the paper to the second person and ask him or her to draw the body of a dinosaur. Do not let the other friends see the drawing.
4. Give the last piece of paper to the third person. Ask him or her to draw the legs and tail of a dinosaur.
5. Tape the the three pieces of paper together to see what kind of dinosaur your friends have made.

Words to Know

climate (KLYE-mit)—the usual weather in a place

dinosaur (DYE-na-sore)—an extinct land reptile; dinosaurs lived on Earth for more than 150 million years.

fossil (FOSS-uhl)—the remains or traces of something that once lived; bones and footprints can be fossils.

herbivore (HUR-buh-vor)—an animal that eats plants

herd (HURD)—a large group of animals; scientists think Iguanodon may have traveled in herds.

paleontologist (PAY-lee-on-TOL-ah-jist)—a scientist who finds and studies fossils

reptile (REP-tile)—a cold-blooded animal with a backbone; scales cover a reptile's body.

scientist (SYE-uhn-tist)—a person who studies the world around us

Read More

Goecke, Michael P. *Iguanodon.* A Buddy Book. Edina, Minn.:
   Abdo, 2002.
Hartzog, Brooke. *Iguanodon and Dr. Gideon Mantell.* Dinosaurs
   and Their Discoverers. New York: PowerKids Press, 1999.
Rodriguez, K. S. *Iguanodon.* Prehistoric Creatures Then and
   Now. Austin, Texas: Steadwell Books, 2000.

Internet Sites

Track down many sites about Iguanodon.
Visit the FACT HOUND at *http://www.facthound.com*

IT IS EASY! IT IS FUN!

1) Go to *http://www.facthound.com*
2) Type in: 0736816232
3) Click on "FETCH IT" and FACT HOUND will find
   several links hand-picked by our editors.

Relax and let our pal FACT HOUND do the research for you!

Index